Night at the Community Center

Nonstandard Measurement

Joshua Rae Martin

Publishing Credits

Dona Herweck Rice, *Editor-in-Chief*; Lee Aucoin, *Creative Director*; Don Tran, *Print Production Manager*; Sara Johnson, *Senior Editor*; Jamey Acosta, *Assistant Editor*; Neri Garcia, *Interior Layout Designer*; Stephanie Reid, *Photo Editor*; Rachelle Cracchiolo, M.A.Ed., *Publisher*

Image Credits

cover Image Source/Getty Images, WLG/Shutterstock; p.1 Image Source/Getty Images, WLG/Shutterstock; p.4 Modesto Bee/Newscom; p.5 (left) gsmad/Shutterstock, (right) Lucian Coman/Shutterstock; p.6 (left) Carrie Devorah/WENN, (right) Forestpath/Shutterstock; p.7 (top) Jupiter Images Corporation, (bottom) Tim Bradley; p.8 (left) ZUMA Press/Newscom, (right) ZUMA Press/Newscom; p.9 ZUMA Press/Newscom; p.10 ZUMA Press/Newscom; p.11 ZTS/Shutterstock; p.12 (left) San Diego Union-Tribune/Newscom, (middle) Patricia Hofmeester/Shutterstock, (right) AGB/Shutterstock; p.13 Aiti/Shutterstock; p.14 Design Pics/Newscom; p.15 Image Source/Getty Images; p.16 (left) Jupiter Images/Newscom, (right) Graça Victoria/Shutterstock; p.17 Frances M. Roberts/Newscom; p.18 (top) Dmitriy Shironosov/Shutterstock, (bottom) Stephanie Reid/Heej/Good Mood Photo/Shutterstock; p.19 (top) ZUMA Press/Newscom, (bottom) Imagine China/Newscom; p.20 (top) ZUMA Press/Newscom, (bottom) Mike Flippo/Shutterstock; p.21 (top) ZUMA Press/Newscom, (bottom) LHF Graphics/Shutterstock; p.22 (left) AFP/Getty Images/Newscom, (right) Aptyp_koK/Shutterstock; p.23 (top) KRT/Newscom, (bottom) Nip/Shutteerstock; p.24 Suzanne Tucker/Shutterstock; p.25 (top) Benis Arapovic/Shutterstock, (bottom) Jaren Jai Wicklund/Shutterstock; p.26 ZUMA Press/Newscom; p.27 Konstantin Sutyagin/Shutterstock; p.29 Patrick Neri/Digital Light Source/Newscom

Teacher Created Materials

5301 Oceanus Drive
Huntington Beach, CA 92649-1030
http://www.tcmpub.com

ISBN 978-1-4333-0428-6
©2011 Teacher Created Materials, Inc.
Reprinted 2013

Table of Contents

Community Center Fun

Friday night can be fun at the **community center**. There are a lot of activities to choose from.

Some people go to classes. Some like the sports.

Classes at the Community Center

These kids like **reptiles**. They are taking a class about snakes.

This boy likes the bull snake. He gets to hold it!

LET'S EXPLORE MATH

This is a picture of the smallest snake in the world. It was discovered in 2008. How many cubes long is this snake?

Some community centers teach how to cook. This class makes easy snacks.

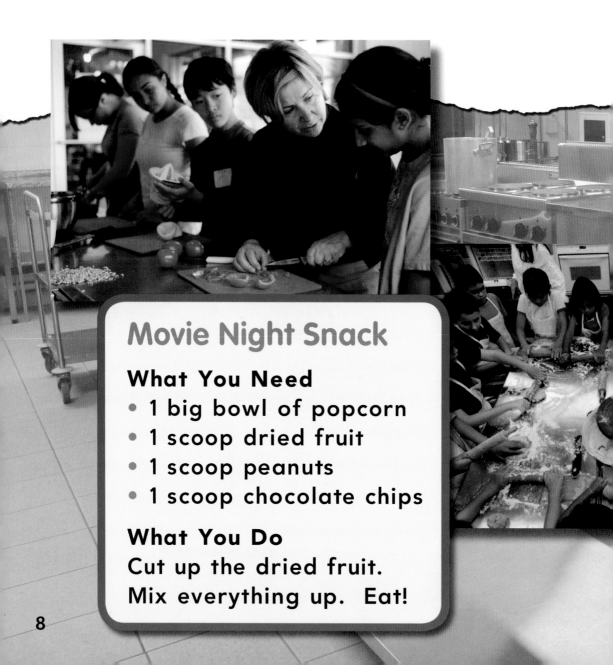

Movie Night Snack

What You Need
- 1 big bowl of popcorn
- 1 scoop dried fruit
- 1 scoop peanuts
- 1 scoop chocolate chips

What You Do
Cut up the dried fruit.
Mix everything up. Eat!

These children are learning how to make cupcakes.

This girl is learning how to give **CPR**.
She practices on a plastic baby.

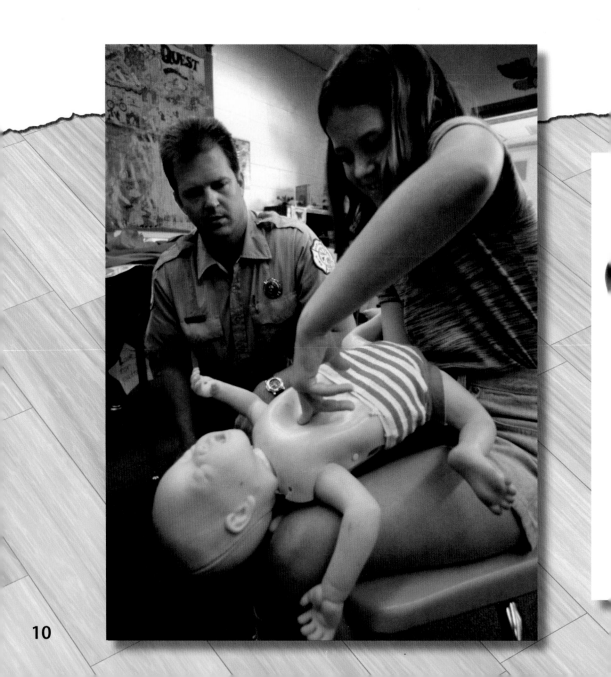

She will also learn about **first aid.**
Her class will make a first-aid kit.

Sports at the Community Center

Some people like to climb. They climb up a special wall.

This climbing wall is tall! How many kids tall is the wall?

These climbers try to make it to the top. The boy gets help from an adult.

Many community centers have a running track.

Most tracks are about a quarter-mile long.

Some runners just want to stay fit. Some use the track to train for races.

These women are taking an exercise class. They use fitness balls in the class.

This teacher can stand on a ball.
That takes good balance!

Lifting weights builds strong bones and muscles. You can start small. Hand weights may weigh just 5 pounds.

LET'S EXPLORE MATH

Which hand weight weighs more?

Barbells can weigh more than 100 pounds!

Liu Chunhong is a weight lifter. She won a gold medal at the 2008 Olympics. She lifted 158 kilograms. That is more than 347 pounds!

Do you like to hit a ball over a net?
Then tennis is a great sport for you.

You can also play **ping pong**. It is a lot like tennis.

LET'S EXPLORE MATH

A tennis racket is big. A ping pong paddle is small. How many ping pong paddles does it take to equal the size of a tennis racket?

Community centers also have basketball courts. Some courts are inside.

Some courts are outside. Many people like to play!

You can **measure** something using your own feet.

a. How many child feet long is the key on this court?

b. How many adult feet long is the key on this court?

c. Are the measurements the same? Why or why not?

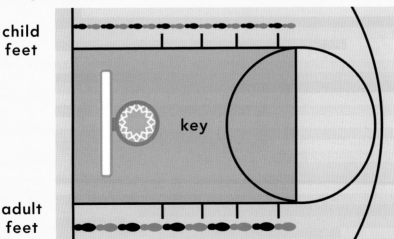

child feet

key

adult feet

23

The pool is a favorite place at a
community center. Some people
swim laps.

Some people play games. Some just relax in the pool.

Some community centers have fun when it gets dark. They show a movie at the pool!

You can find lots of fun things to
do at the community center!

Feeding Animals

Jack helps out at the zoo during the summer. He has to choose the containers that are used to feed the animals. He looks at the chart for help.

What the Animals Eat

Animal	Food	Container
pythons	small mice	
hummingbirds	sugar and water mix	
polar bears	fish	
kangaroos	plant pellets	
elephants	leaves	

This is his list of containers.

- 1 garbage can
- 1 bucket
- 1 bottle
- 1 small pan
- 1 large bowl

What container should be used to feed each animal? Copy the chart. Choose which container could hold each type of food.

Solve It!

Use the steps below to help you solve the problem.

Step 1: Think about what each animal eats.

Step 2: Think about what can go into each container. For example, which container would best hold fish?

Step 3: Think about the size of the animals. If they are big animals, they need big containers.

Step 4: Choose a container for each animal. Then fill in the chart.

Glossary

community center—a place where people can learn, exercise, and have fun

CPR—a type of first aid given when a person stops breathing

first aid—treatment of minor injuries, or pretreatment of major injuries before getting help from a doctor

measure—the use of standard or nonstandard units to find the size of an object

ping pong—a game played on a table by two or four people with a hollow ball and paddles

reptiles—animals that prefer warm climates and have dry, scaly skin

Index

Let's Explore Math

Page 7:
10 cubes

Page 12:
8 kids tall

Page 18:
hand weight A

Page 21:
3 ping pong paddles

Page 23:
a. 16 child feet long
b. 10 adult feet long
c. No, the adult feet are larger than the child feet.

Solve the Problem

What the Animals Eat

Animal	Food	Container
pythons	small mice	small pan
hummingbirds	sugar and water mix	bottle
polar bears	fish	bucket
kangaroos	plant pellets	large bowl
elephants	leaves	garbage can